FEARLESS

A 30-DAY DEVOTIONAL
TO ENCOURAGE YOUR LIFE

Mike Sternad

FEARLESS
A 30-DAY DEVOTIONAL TO ENCOURAGE YOUR LIFE

By Mike Sternad

Published by Contented Life Publishing

Mailing Address: 312 T Schillinger Rd. S,
Mobile, Alabama 36608

Website: www.calvarychapelmobile.com
Email: mikesternad@gmail.com

Copyright © 2021 by Mike Sternad

First edition.

All rights reserved. No part of this publication may be reproduced, stored in a retrieval system, or transmitted in any form or by any means without the express written consent of Mike Sternad.

Unless otherwise indicated, Scripture quotations in this book are taken from the New King James Version of the Bible. Copyright © 1979, 1980, 1982 by Thomas Nelson, Inc., Publishers. Used by permission.

Edited by Miriam Rogers
Cover Design by Ashley Garcia
Interior Design by Ulrika Towgood

ISBN 978-1-7343454-5-2

Printed in the United States of America

This book is dedicated to my awesome wife, Brianne, who was all in with me to follow God's call, moving across the country from California to the Deep South to plant a church and start a whole new life. She is fearless and an amazing support.
I love you so much!

TABLE OF CONTENTS

FOREWORD 7

INTRODUCTION 9

DAY 1 **FEAR NOT** 13

DAY 2 **BE BRAVE** 16

DAY 3 **TRULY TRUST** 19

DAY 4 **BE ON GUARD** 22

DAY 5 **SEEK PERMANENT PEACE** 25

DAY 6 **FORSAKE ALL FEARS** 28

DAY 7 **ENDING UNEASINESS** 31

DAY 8 **YOU ARE HIS** 34

DAY 9 **COURAGE** 37

DAY 10 **PRESENT PROVISION** 40

DAY 11 **CAST YOUR CARES** 43

DAY 12 **NO FEAR** 46

DAY 13 **HIS PRESENCE** 49

DAY 14 **NOT ALONE** 52

DAY 15 **CRUSH FEAR** 55

TABLE OF CONTENTS (Continued)

DAY 16 **CALM AND QUIET** 58

DAY 17 **ONLY BELIEVE** 61

DAY 18 **DON'T BE TROUBLED** 64

DAY 19 **OVERARCHING PEACE** 67

DAY 20 **SAVED FROM SINKING** 71

DAY 21 **UNDOING FEAR** 74

DAY 22 **FORGET EARTHLY FEAR** 77

DAY 23 **GENUINE REST** 80

DAY 24 **SECURE IN HIM** 83

DAY 25 **FERVENT FAITH** 86

DAY 26 **BE FEARLESS** 89

DAY 27 **A SETTLED HEART** 92

DAY 28 **WIPE OUT WORRY** 95

DAY 29 **FOREVER FEARLESS** 98

DAY 30 **GOD IS WITH YOU** 101

CONCLUSION 104

FOREWORD

> *"Fear not, for I am with you; be not dismayed, for I am your God. I will strengthen you, yes, I will help you, I will uphold you with My righteous right hand." Isaiah 41:10*

Much of my life was spent in the sport of boxing. I began learning the *sweet science* at only three years old and left the sport as a pro at twenty-six. I fought on Showtime, ESPN and HBO. I've had almost 200 fights and my pro record was 22-3 with sixteen KO's. My fight name was the Xtreme Machine.

As you might expect, many fans and friends often think I'm fearless, but that couldn't be further from the truth. I've heard it said before, "Machines don't get scared." But truthfully, I'm not a machine; I'm human just like you and I've struggled with fear since my earliest memories.

I was afraid as a little boy, abused, manipulated and mistreated. I was afraid to fail and I was afraid of rejection. I was afraid I wouldn't fit in and I was afraid that no one liked me. I was afraid of being alone.

My early years were wrecked with fear, and as I approached forty it still lied around every corner waiting to strangle the life out of me. This is the nature of fear. There's always something to be afraid of. But fear only has the power you allow it to have. As Franklin D. Roosevelt once said, "The only thing we have to fear is fear itself."

In *Fearless*, Mike clearly points us to the only unfailing eradicator of fear—the Almighty, the Prince of Peace, the Great I Am, Yahweh, Yeshua...Jesus! In this devotional we are shown that we can replace fear with trust, and to trust in the One who is trustworthy! We can find strength and courage in Him!

> Ebo Elder
> Founder of Reality Ministries
> Author of *The Great Comeback*

INTRODUCTION

Fear is a faith stopper and can do some damage to your mindset and perspective. When you allow fear to freely reign in your heart and life, you lose sight of the Father and end up fending for yourself. Fear can cause the strongest person to be weakened to the point of inactivity and immobility. The fact is that fear will never further or foster your walk with God; there will never be progress when fear is involved.

Many believers have failed to live out the calling of God because they let fear have the last word. What are some ways we can make fear fall away from us? What action do we need to take to eradicate fear on a daily basis? The simple answer is to build our faith. Faith is the main factor that will destroy and defeat fear. Not just faith in faith but faith in the Lord who is all-powerful and can defeat any worry, anxiety or fear that may stealthily creep into your life. Faith in our Father and the Lord Jesus Christ is what needs to dictate our decisions and direct our God-given path in this life. Faith will lead to a fearlessness that is unstoppable. When fear begins to invade our mind, we must give that fear over to God and feed our faith and saturate our soul with the truth from the Scriptures!

Before I was a believer I would seriously let fear run rampant in my heart and mind. Expectations that I felt society had placed on me caused worry to bubble to the surface of my life. If it were not for my faith in the Lord, I would not have the heavenly peace that I now have as I walk with God. Faith helps me forge ahead in a world that fosters, promotes and pushes society toward fear.

Our focus will determine whether we live in fear or walk by faith. The first devotional that I ever wrote was called *Focus*. I was called by God to write on that subject to help people focus on Jesus in a world that is overloaded with distractions and temptations. It sounds so simple, but the truth is that we will have faith in whatever we focus on. So if I'm honed in on my circumstances and I let my tough situations dictate my day, I will be a wreck! If I focus on a human being and attempt to find my faith in that person, I will be disappointed, let down and depressed! But if I focus on the Lord Jesus and have faith in His will and His plan, the result will be a lack of fear and an influx of faith! Your focus is the starting point that leads to either timidity or triumph, and determine your level of faith. When your eyes are upon the Lord, the result will be strengthened faith and steadfastness that this world cannot build within you. Only God can do that work. Also, when you focus on the truth from God, you won't worry about your job, your family or your future. When your focus is on the eternal, you will not be a victim—you will be victorious!

You can spend your time anxious and stressed, or you can spend your life resting on and believing in the beautiful promises of God. There is nothing to be anxious about and there is no need to worry about possible future events and things that *could* happen. Focus on Jesus and plant your feet right where the Lord has you now. Buckle down and fill your soul with the Word of God and the result will be a heavenly resolve and fortified faith.

Faith puts to death the storms that rage within and the anxiety that sprints forth from the hypothetical situations we let ruminate in our minds. Let those thoughts go, give them to God and be free! We have every reason to be bold and courageous in this world and there is no reason to be ashamed about being confident in Christ and courageous in our everyday life. After all, what an awesome witness for the Lord!

God calls you to be confident in Him every step of the way. Rise up and move forward in your faith, factoring out any and all fear. Allow your faith to propel you forward from now to eternity. My prayer is that as you journey through *Fearless*, you will allow fear to fall to the ground and be left to die. May you be encouraged to forsake fear as you focus on the Father and walk by faith.

DAY 1
FEAR NOT

"For God has not given us a spirit of fear, but of power and of love and of a sound mind."
2 Timothy 1:7

Let fear fall to the ground, stomp on it confidently and walk away. Fear is not from the Father and timidity should not occupy any part of who you are as a believer. God has called *you* to walk by faith and forge ahead in the calling He has for you. The Lord has and will equip you for every adventure He calls you to! If there is even a hint of fear that creeps into your life, take action and turn over that fear to God. Determine that fear is not welcome to take residence in your mind. Let. fear. fall.

Paul wrote the above exhortation to Timothy because as a leader of the church Timothy faced fear. One of the most repetitive and comforting phrases in the Bible is, "Do not be afraid." I'm actually extremely comforted right now just typing this true phrase from the Scriptures! Presently, the Coronavirus has wreaked havoc on the world, our nation, and our community. A lot of insecurity and worry has emanated from this pesky virus. But as we read the Bible, the Lord uses the Scriptures to bring instant comfort to our hearts and bright hope to our lives!

When we let fear in, the result will be a whirlwind of anxiety; an unsettled outlook that pervades our lives. Fear is not of the Lord, nor will it ever be from the Lord. He doesn't send fear our way to see how we would deal with it or to see how strong we really are. God's not a hater, or pusher of worry. Yes, this is Christianity 101 but it's true—the way to deal with fear is to pray. You might say, "No, that's too simple, there must be something else I should do." Or, "Praying is nice and all but maybe if I talk to people or go to the gym or write in my journal, then everything will be fine and fear will go away." These actions are all good and helpful but the first thing we must always do is pray to our powerful God! Fear will flail in the wind when we pray for an increased faith because the fact is that fear comes from below, faith comes from above. We cannot let fear rear its ugly head into our life circumstances. May we constantly pray for our faith to be increased so as to decrease the existence of anxiety in our lives.

> Fear is super weak when it's set beside the truth that God is amazingly strong.

I think it's important to know the heart of God and the capabilities of God. As we read the Bible every day, we get to know the loving heart of our Father, and we grow to understand how God uses His power to protect us from irrational emotions that the enemy hurls our way—namely, fear! Power, love and a sound mind are God-given components that crowd out the fear which emanates from the world, the enemy and our flesh. The epic truth is that the power of God will peel away any and all worry, protecting us from the invasion of fear. The love of God will annihilate anxiety as we have the assurance of knowing His love calms the storm of worry within us. First John 4:18 says, "Perfect love casts out fear." God's love puts to death the fear that can secretly creep into our mind when we cease to be aware of our spiritual surroundings.

Paul writes about the Lord giving believers a sound mind. A sound mind means we are sober and serious and clear of any form of fear. When it comes to faith and fear, we must take it super seriously because they can either make us or break us. Let your heart be settled right now knowing that power, love and a sound mind comes from the Lord and He wants to fill you with these.

May the calm heart of your Creator result in a powerful and prominent peace in your life. God never wants you to be fearful, afraid or unsure about anything! He isn't sitting up in heaven waiting for an opportunity to mess with you just because. Instead, the Lord wants to settle your heart, protect your mind, and give you peace and rest in your soul! As you live your life for the Lord, give your anxiety over to Him as much as it takes. He does not want you to sit in a pool of worry and freak out over all the *what if* questions in your life. You are not called to hone in on those questions about future events that you're not even sure about. Listen, God is sure about your future and He knows how to lift you up and flood you with real peace. Know and believe that fear doesn't come from the Father. Power comes from your Provider and love comes from the Lord. A sound mind comes from your Maker. So remember, fear not, God is with you.

DAY 2
BE BRAVE

> *"Behold, the virgin shall be with child, and bear a Son, and they shall call His name Immanuel," which is translated, "God with us."*
> Matthew 1:23

When you fully realize God is always with you, worry will be a thing of the past. Knowing that God's presence is perpetual in your life should lift up your heart to a plane of joy and result in heavenly comfort. Can you believe that the Lord loves you, cares for you and is with you for all of your time on this earth? Talk about mind blowing! The Lord isn't just hanging out at church waiting for a visiting hour with you, He goes with you as long as you follow Him! Do not let any distance get between you and the Lord; instead, stay in lock step with your Creator so that fear will dissipate.

My mind can be a busy place to visit and often I have to cut off some thoughts and let the Lord take the stress away. I love going on vacation but not to places that are tourist traps. Those places are not relaxing and comforting to me at all. My idea of relaxing is going to a quiet place where I can just take a breath and enjoy sunny days with my family. Similarly, our mind can be cluttered and busy and before we know it, we are dismayed over a thought or hypothetical scenario and we cease to find rest. The fact is, God is with us; therefore, we have no excuse to let anxiety get the best of who we are! *Dismay* means "to be broken down in courage." God doesn't break us down or tempt us to the brink of discouragement—He builds us up through the Holy Spirit, prayer, and His Word! God's presence brings protection and results in the eradication of fear. A. B. Simpson wrote, "Fear is born of Satan, and if we would only take time to think a moment we would see that everything Satan says is founded upon a falsehood."

Not only does the Lord expose the lies of the enemy and extract fear from our lives, He also instills His strength within us.

> Dismay can be kicked out of our mind and into the dirt for the Lord wants our hearts to be completely courageous.

Our God takes away our negative outlook on life and blesses us with positive promises from His Word. The Lord adds to our lives the characteristics that make us more than conquerors (Romans 8:37), and He blesses us with the emphatic assurance of His presence. We can believe and trust that the Lord upholds us every moment of every day because God has never been a promise breaker. He is our God and He *will* uphold us every step of the way. We don't have to strive or struggle in our own strength to conjure up true courage to face our daily trials. The beautiful reality is that it is solely God's work to strengthen and hold us up. We simply see progressing spiritual motion when we realize God's continual presence, resulting in the falling away of fear from our very lives.

Know that the presence of the Lord in your life leads to the absence of fear. If you are struggling with worry, begin to focus more on the Lord's presence and gain strength by leaning upon Him. Being conscious of His presence will bring an intense bravery to your heart and life and keep you on the path of truth. God is amazing at giving you the confidence you need to face the daily challenges that arise. The key to courage is to remember and revel in the fact that God is with you wherever you go. The enemy is weak and already defeated. Don't give in to His lies and don't let his whispers of deceit affect your mind. God said it, you can believe it!

DAY 3
TRULY TRUST

"Whenever I am afraid, I will trust in You."
Psalm 56:3

You can pretend that you aren't afraid, but you'd be lying to yourself. There are things that scare you. There are events that freak you out. The question is, what is the immediate step following the infiltration of fear? The fact is that fear and worry will come and knock on the door of your mind. Fear has your number and is waiting to invade you with his friends, Anxiety and Stress. The amazing truth is that the way to eradicate fear as it rears its ugly head in your life is to trust in God. Trusting God will tear away worry and bring an influx of faith into your heart, mind and life. So annihilate the feeling of fear by trusting in the Father.

There are a couple more questions we can ask ourselves to assess how we would deal with fear when it shows up. Will we let everything get to us and tear down our determined boldness? Or will we trust God to change our fear into unstoppable faith? If we overthink every single detail of every aspect of our lives, we will be filled with worry and feel constantly overwhelmed. Those moments when I stress out the most are the same moments where I keep thinking about the hypotheticals in life and the scenarios based on the *what-ifs*. They only bring worry and insecurity. The truth is that there are many things that could go wrong, yet most of those negative outcomes will never come to pass.

Trusting in God can tear fear in two causing its grip to loosen in our lives. The more years that go by, the more I learn that trusting in God on a regular and consistent basis leaves no room for fear to reside in me. Obedience, faith, trust and belief are synonyms that make up what our action should be as Christians.

Jesus made it really simple. After He prayed all night, He saw Simon and Andrew and simply said, "Follow me." He didn't say follow fear or worry about everything because the flesh likes that. He didn't say follow the trends or what's popular. He didn't say follow your feelings and just do what you want to do. He simply said, "Follow Me."

> Fear will diminish and dissolve when we are too busy trusting the Lord.

Trusting God is a terrific way to transform fear into faith. But when fear is leading our lives, then everything seems unsure and we have no clue what is going to happen. It can be scary and fear can lead to stress and unhealthy habits and seriously bad decisions.

There may have been times in your life when you let fear lead and the result was major anxiety and serious burnout. You have to ask yourself, what good is fear going to do in my life? The answer to that question is fear will yield no positive results. Ever. Trusting God is the avenue to a victorious Christian life. Period. If you've been walking with the Lord for a long time, you know this truth. Yet, there can tend to be a gap between what we know and what we do. Wisdom is one small step further than knowledge. So why is it so hard to take that step? It's so hard to take that step because that step requires the motivation of faith and the will to act upon heavenly fact! And faith is saying I will trust God even and especially when I do not see all the details and I don't know the full story.

Fear is conquered as our minds are constantly placed on the One who calms the storm inside of us. External life events can easily cause fear and anxiety to well up within us. Yet, the Lord can easily cause fear to flee as we consistently trust in Him.

For you to truly trust in the Lord is to have faith to the extent that every single fear in your mind is silenced. Whenever you feel worry begin to creep into an unguarded area of your life, recognize it but don't dwell in it. Instead, allow your trust in God to guard your heart and tackle those fears to the ground. Let your faith pin down those fears to the mat. Your fear is never as powerful as your faith. Never. Fear is from beneath but faith is from God. Focus on the Lord and the result will be built up faith and a powerful security in Him. It's time to let your faith overpower any and all fear that you will face. The way to be totally free of fear is to fully trust the God who can make fear fall for good. Let it fall and leave it there. As fear tries to rise, confidently walk away and don't look back.

DAY 4
BE ON GUARD

> *"Be anxious for nothing, but in everything by prayer and supplication, with thanksgiving, let your requests be made known to God; and the peace of God, which surpasses all understanding, will guard your hearts and minds through Christ Jesus."* Philippians 4:6-7

Praying to the Lord is the action that you can take to curb nervousness and axe anxiety. There may have been some serious complications in your life when it comes to *worry, anxiety* and *stress*. This three-man team is designed by the enemy to strangle your trust in God, question the Lord and live in fear. So how are you supposed to make it all go away? Pray. You've heard it before and you'll hear it again and the answer may even frustrate you. But the fact is when you pray, what's complicated becomes simple. Praying to your all-powerful God will flatten fear, annihilate anxiety and wash worry away.

Praying brings a divine comfort that cannot come from anywhere or anyone else other than God. A great pastor and commentator, Warren Wiersbe, said, "Fill your mind with the truth of the Word and your heart with prayer, and trust God to take care of you."[1] Being aware of God's presence will bring a heightened rest, a calm mind and long-lasting

---

[1] Warren Wiersbe, *Prayer, Praise & Promises: A Daily Walk Through the Psalms.* (Grand Rapids, MI: Baker Books), 2011.

and genuine peace. As anxiety results from unsure times, prayer results in peace and protection. Our external world should not cause anxiety, it should cause alignment with our Lord. Life is really a series of contrasts. As we see the world growing darker, we can shine brighter for the Lord. As things seem to be so bad around us, we are reminded that God is so good. Praying and connecting with our Creator will put up hedges of help from the One who is with us always.

> Prayer is the action that impacts our lives in the form of peace, rest and comfort.

Our hearts will be guarded as we consistently seek the Lord in the midst of the world's madness. Part of my testimony is that I had gone to some less than prestigious institutions. Every time I walked into a new institution I would be incredibly nervous and stressed. Being aware of our surroundings can bring out the worst kind of worry and lure us away from the Lord.

When I first taught the Bible at a church that was different from what I was accustomed, I was so nervous. I needed to pray before that moment like never before because I was worried like never before.

To be fearless is to be free of unwarranted worry. It is so disheartening to think about how much time we have spent worrying about stuff that never actually happened! Our minds can cause our hearts a massive amount of destructive stress when we leave prayer out of the equation of our lives. When I was going to college I absolutely hated math. I've hated it my entire life. So when a math test was scheduled, my world became quite a bit dimmer. The day of the test I would go somewhere private before class started, pull out my NIV pocket Bible and read Philippians 4:6-7 and pray. It was the only way to curb my anxiety for the horribly difficult questions I would have to answer!

We need to seek the Lord so that our hearts and minds are guarded, protected and at rest. The enemy loves to take a calm situation and make it seem overly chaotic. He loves to take what is simple and complicate it to the point of intense stress. He floods our minds with discouragement and doubt. He introduces skepticism and fabricated scenarios in order to cause a large amount of insecurity. When our minds are on sketchy situations, it can seem scary but when our minds are on our Maker, we will have complete protection from those feelings of fear. Prayer is the cure.

Be on guard and realize that prayer is a weapon that brings total protection from feelings of insecurity and doubt. The road to peace in the midst of the storms of life begin and end with prayer. Stay in prayer on a consistent basis and make it a healthy spiritual habit. Don't leave prayer out, or else worry and fear will be added to your life. Remember that God is the guard who stands at the door of your heart and brings peace like no one else can. The Almighty is the One who kicks anxiety out the door and tames our troubled hearts. Seeking God through prayer is the key to keep anxiety at bay.

DAY 5
SEEK PERMANENT PEACE

"Peace I leave with you, My peace I give to you; not as the world gives do I give to you. Let not your heart be troubled, neither let it be afraid."
John 14:27

You may have been searching for heart peace in all the wrong places. You tried to find peace in people, in situations, material items or even success. Yet, you realized over and over that peace cannot be found on this earth. The source of peace for a fallen humanity is the Prince of Peace—Jesus. In Jesus you have rest, peace and relief that only He can provide. Peace on this earth is just a temporary reprieve but peace from Jesus is permanent and eternal. What a blessing!

This verse struck a chord in my soul when my heart was in turmoil years ago. My soon-to-be wife, Brianne, had it written on a full-length mirror in her bedroom. I looked it up and was amazed at this claim of Jesus that He is the peace that I needed. Since that moment, John 14:27 has come up over and over in my heart when chaos began to invade. How many times have we searched for a glimmer of peace only to find turmoil and temporary heart rest? When Jesus became the focal point of my life, peace resulted giving me a relief that I had never before experienced.

I truly believe that people want peace in their hearts, but their focus is blurry. Clarity came for me when I realized that Christ is my peace in a general everyday sense! Jesus gives us a calm heart rest that seems foreign to the world because they don't understand what true peace really is. No one does until they begin walking with and living for Jesus. Watchman Nee said, "A born-again person ought to possess unspeakable peace in the spirit."[2]

The world will give a fabricated, artificial kind of peace which is really striving masked in calmness. I lived that way for years and years and it was such a struggle! But when I surrendered to Christ and began living for Him, everything changed. Sure, my circumstances were still rough at times but I had peace in my heart and it made all the difference in my life.

> True peace isn't found in your journey on this earth; true peace emanates from God to His kids.

We will face trials and troubles throughout our lives because we are sinners in a fallen world, living with other sinners. There will be strife and turmoil but there will also be permanent peace in our hearts when Jesus resides there. Many people are going through some kind of hardship right now and they are lost, confused and wandering. They are looking for reprieve and relief but they are looking in the wrong places. This is why as Christians, we are

---

[2] Watchman Nee, *The Spiritual Man*. (New York, NY: Christian Fellowship Publishers), 1968.

always talking about Jesus because not only is He our rescuer, He is our source of rest! Troubles will rise but we can stand assured that peace will rise much higher. Fear is a tactic that the enemy uses but it is *not* effective against the love of Jesus and the power of God. We can drive through difficulties and tear through trials when we truly acknowledge and receive the peace of Jesus.

Remember that the trial you are facing right now cannot touch the peace that is freely gifted to you. Problems will show up periodically in your life, but they cannot eliminate the heart rest that stems from Jesus. Rest assured that the Lord Jesus is with you through every storm, asleep on a pillow because He is in control of it all. You have no need to worry and fret because Jesus in your heart will crowd out any and all fears that will arise. God is stronger than any troubled situation that you may face. Receive the peace that comes from the Lord Jesus who absolutely loves you. Know that He has you every single day!

DAY 6
FORSAKE ALL FEARS

> *"There is no fear in love; but perfect love casts out fear, because fear involves torment. But he who fears has not been made perfect in love."*
> 1 John 4:18

Your palms are sweating and your heartbeat races. You are scared out of your mind and wonder if there is ever a point where fear will fade. Worry has built up and the moment comes and passes and you realize you worried for absolutely no reason! Pretty anti-climactic, right? This may happen often in your life. These fears about what could happen lead to worry and before you know it, you are freaking out! Don't worry though, there's a cure.

Fear brings nothing but torment, stress and turmoil which seem endless; feelings that a rational person would not hope for. Before I was walking with the Lord, I would sit alone in my bed at night thinking about death. That doesn't sound like fun, right? But I wondered what would happen when I die. *Is it just nothingness? I don't want that!* I would think myself scared and one time I remember just trembling with a sense of hopelessness. When I began my journey on the road of God's will, all my questions were immediately answered as I traveled through the gospels gaining insight into life, death and eternity. God's Word eradicated my fear when I realized that the love of

God is powerful enough to trample trepidation to the point of total assurance and security.

Many people have questions in relation to fear like, how do I cast out fear? How do I destroy and get rid of the fear in my life? The answer is actually very succinct. Perfect love pummels fear and tears apart trepidation. God's love is that powerful. The Father's love is the most magnificent agent to kill fear and rip apart worry. Not only does God love us but God *is* love. So as we gaze our eyes toward God, fear will be cast out, timidity and worry will be eradicated and anxiety will disappear. The agonizing will actually turn into adoration. Worry will turn into worship. Fear will turn into faith.

> God has no association with fear besides having the power through love to annihilate it.

To be made perfect in love means to revel and rest in God's affection toward us to the point of awe. Fear can paralyze us but the Father's love brings peace, solace and repose. Fear can cause our attitude to fluctuate and be completely erratic, but the Father's love causes freedom and relief from anxiety. The Bible makes it crystal clear that we as believers are to revere God and nothing or no one else. Fearing God has everything to do with standing in a posture of praise and knowing that God is absolutely powerful and in control. The Lord doesn't use His power to abuse, He uses His power to love! God's perfect love will so overwhelm your fear that fear will actually quickly flee your heart, mind and life. William Gurnall said, "The chains of love are stronger than the chains of fear."[3] Soak in the love of God and watch as your fear detaches from your mind and is replaced with solid faith.

God calls you to stand firm in the faith so that fear will not invade. He wants you to forsake every fear and therefore focus on His perfect love. God is not in the business of causing you to be worried or anxious about any situation that you are facing. Fear is always from the enemy who wants to stunt any spiritual growth in your walk with God. Keep seeking the Lord and walking by faith and you will be free, relieved and at rest! If you have been fearful because of a certain situation you are currently in, lay those fears at the feet of Jesus. Don't let the enemy get the best of you and don't let worry whisk away the faith that has been built up in your heart by your powerful God! Cast those fears into the fiery furnace and leave them there to burn. God's love is powerful enough to save a soul and deliver you from every single one of your earthly fears.

---

[3] https://heraldofhiscoming.org/index.php/read-the-herald/past-issues/262-past-issues/2001/aug01/3138-god-s-word-judges-god-s-word-relieves-8-01

DAY 7
ENDING UNEASINESS

"In the multitude of my anxieties within me, Your comforts delight my soul." Psalm 94:19

As we sojourn through this earth, worry can begin to build up and we may begin to heavily fear because we go through severe hardships. Anxieties begin externally and end up internally affecting us. You have moments where you're worried about the future; whether you are going to be OK or not. You may be in a situation that has caused you to question whether you are in the right place doing the right thing. Here is what you must remember: The Lord is the only One who can bring comfort to your life and delight your very soul. This world will cause you to be anxious and afraid but just remember to keep your eyes on the Almighty God for comfort, relief and solace.

Authentic comfort does not come from this world, from people, from material items or from situations. We've all saved up our money to finally buy some new product that we were looking forward to owning. This was our dream and finally we have this thing, whatever it is! And it's exciting at first and we are pumped to own it and use it and the thrill is strong. But then some time goes by and this product loses its flair and the momentum of fulfillment is waning. This item that was supposed to fulfill doesn't really bring satisfaction to us anymore. So on to the next thing! Authentic comfort and true consolation come from God alone as He has the power to do away with anxieties. Our carnal expectations are often crushed when we place our hope in the earthly rather than in eternity. But when we place our hope in the Lord, worry begins to dissipate and our apt response is to worship Him. When uneasiness comes, may we call upon our Almighty God for He is our comfort, He is our delight, and He is where we can find perfect peace in the midst of the mess called the world. Charles Spurgeon said, "Anxiety does not empty tomorrow of its sorrows, but only empties today of its strength." Anxieties will dissolve as long as we depend upon and trust in the Lord. It is possible to have comfort and joy even as we are going through serious hardships.

> Comfort only comes when your eyes are focused on your heavenly Father.

The most difficult times in my life happened when I was *not* walking with God and doing my own thing. The most confusing and uncomfortable times in my life was when I was a believer but distant from Him. The Lord didn't move away from me, I moved away from Him. The world grabbed hold of me and I let the storms of life knock me down. When I am avidly following Jesus and placing every ounce of trust in Him, my faith is established on the solid Rock and will not crumble. I can smile through a storm as long as I keep my feet firmly planted upon the foundation that is Christ. And if it's not enough that God takes away severe anxiety, He also replaces anxiety with amazing serenity. Being a believer doesn't mean everything goes well all the time, but it does mean as we go through the storm, we can still have serenity, solace, peace and security. God holds us close through the most heart-wrenching hardships.

As you navigate through this fallen world, remember that uneasiness ends when we hold onto the Lord. Anxiety will cease and fearlessness will increase as you bend your heart toward the Savior of the world. You will be filled with delight by depending upon God in every season and every circumstance you find yourself in. You may have trials that seem constant and you may be so anxiety-filled because of those trials. When storms rage around you, remember that God is the source of comfort and true peace. As you seek God, not only will you be comforted, He will give you delight through the darkest times. He has you. Keep your eyes upon the eternal so as to enter into His comfort.

DAY 8
YOU ARE HIS

"But now, thus says the LORD, who created you, O Jacob, and He who formed you, O Israel: 'Fear not, for I have redeemed you; I have called you by your name, You are Mine.'" Isaiah 43:1

You belong to someone. You had a mom and a dad, and whether you had a great upbringing or a tough childhood, the fact is that you had parents. When you began walking with the Lord, surrendering yourself to Him and His ways, you became a child of God. Now you belong to Him. This is good news because God's heart toward you is not hard; rather it is gentle and incredibly loving. Revel in the fact that you belong to the Lord and He absolutely loves you!

Knowing that Christians belong to the Lord is enough to rid any child of God of fear. In today's verse, we know that the people of Judah had every plausible reason to be afraid of Babylon's army and their possible exile. It was scary and had caused many of these people to worry and fret for the future. Yet, the Lord identifies Himself as their Creator and Redeemer. There is something supernaturally comforting to know that God is the One who created us, redeemed us and currently sustains us.

I know for certain that I don't have to live my life in fear or unwarranted anxiety because of God's heart toward me. He is protecting me, holding me and helping me every single day and every step of the way. Pastor Charles Stanley said, "We can be tired, weary and emotionally distraught, but after spending time alone with God, we find that He injects into our bodies energy, power and strength."[4] I've been rescued from this world, from myself and from the enemy who regularly attempts to lure me away from all that is right and true. Our Father in heaven who lovingly created us is the One who can easily keep us calm through any conflict and storm. The reality is that our Redeemer has already rescued us from anything that can harm our soul or break down our faith. We are blessed to continue on with Him, keeping our eyes fixed on Jesus. There is literally no need to worry.

> God loves you more than you can comprehend and fathom.

The Lord, who calls us by name, knows every detail about our lives. This means that God, our Creator, Redeemer and Rescuer, is personal and wants us to knit our hearts with His. I have never been a good heart sharer and even after all these years of marriage, I'm still learning and reminding myself that I need to share my heart with my wife on a regular basis. It's not that I don't want to personally share with her, it's that I just need to be reminded to engage in a conversation with the amazing woman that God has blessed me with. The same is true with our relationship with the Lord. He wants us to engage with Him and communicate what we are

---

[4] Charles Stanley, *How to Listen to God* (Nashville, TN: Thomas Nelson), 2002.

facing and what we are going through. The beautiful thing is that the Lord wants to hear from our heart what we are going through and what we need help with. He knows who we are and what we struggle with but He wants us to talk it out with Him and be honest with Him. I also believe He wants us to know exactly who He is and what His heart toward us is like. The more we peer into God's Word, the clearer the character of God will become to us. God wants to be known by those He created and as we seek Him and pursue the Lord, we will get to know His heart and realize His great love and beautiful grace on such a deeper and more intimate level.

The Lord created you out of love. He will protect and guard your soul in the most intense and chaotic situations. The Lord is your Redeemer and He wants to give you rest from that irritating fear that you can't seem to shake. God's *not* calling you to be afraid and filled with anxiety all the time. He is calling you to trust Him and as a result of trusting Him, you will have heart rest and lasting peace. God loves you, and as you communicate with Him and pursue His calling for your life, you will be in a good spiritual place growing toward Him rather than away from Him. Believe that He is always there to help. Daily reach out to Him in the midst of scary storms, compounded conflicts or terrible trials. Hit fear in the face with this fact: You are His.

DAY 9
COURAGE

"Have I not commanded you? Be strong and of good courage; do not be afraid, nor be dismayed, for the LORD your God is with you wherever you go." Joshua 1:9

God will give you courage and boldness for the mission that He has for you. The Lord knows what reassurances and encouragements you need from day to day and season to season. Courage and boldness do not emanate from within; they come from above. As the Lord leads you, He will equip you with traits that will ignite a passion to fulfill His perfect and amazing purposes. When God tells you to be strong and not be afraid, you can trust His words and heed His ways! He is your protector, provider and prime encourager.

Joshua was entering a new season of life as he was called to take over some major responsibilities. He would replace Moses who was a renowned leader; some would have said Moses was irreplaceable. It reminds me of when one lead pastor resigns and a new pastor steps up and takes over. Often there are people who feel they cannot stay at the church because the new pastor doesn't teach like their old pastor. I'm thankful that the Lord called me to start a church from the ground up rather than taking over an existing church! But there are certain expectations and when people see change, usually most get skittish and question everything, or they get worried and leave.

So Joshua was called to lead a whole nation of people into the promised land. God doesn't command us to do something unless there is a need. In other words, God told Joshua to be courageous because he was afraid and probably a bit overwhelmed at the prospect of going from Moses' assistant to the main leader! Joshua needed God's encouraging promises to prevent fear from welling up inside of him and causing doubt and timidity. The Lord knows our hearts and He understands how fear can hinder any purposeful progress. If fear is a part of our daily lives, we will not be living fully for the Lord and we'll let how we feel dictate what we do. Being scared will put a stop to any spiritual momentum that we have built up in our hearts and lives. We must turn to His reassuring promises from His perfect Word.

Fear does not have the last word in your life.

The Lord tells Joshua to not be afraid, even though he was facing what we'd perceive as impossible obstacles. What we perceive as trials, God sees as unobstructed trails. We simply need to trust that if He has called us to something, He will make a way and give us all we need to move forward and progress in the calling He has for us.

In 2017 I was so excited to move from Los Angeles to Mobile, Alabama with my wife and two daughters.

I knew for sure God called me to start Calvary Chapel Mobile. The Lord gave me amazing and pointed promises to prepare me up to the time when we packed the car and drove thirty hours to start a new life. Without those promises I would have been completely freaked out.

As the Lord leads you He will give you those comforting promises that will prepare you for what's ahead so that you don't have to be dismayed. The word *dismayed* actually means "to be terrified or shattered." As we step out in faith for the Lord, we can ask Him to terminate terror and hold us together as we steadily walk by faith. The fact is fear will shatter us; faith will shelter us. As we actively live out what God has put into our hearts, we stay centered in the middle of His mission for us with boldness and courage. The comforting truth is that the Lord keeps us safe and equips us for every excursion He calls us to.

God doesn't want you to be timid and scared or to back down from what He has called you to do. From day to day and season to season you can emphatically know that your Creator is equipping you presently for what He has for you in the future. He is protecting you every step of the way and will provide everything you need to fulfill your divine mission. He was with you, is with you, and will be with you wherever you go.

DAY 10
PRESENT PROVISION

"Therefore do not worry about tomorrow, for tomorrow will worry about its own things. Sufficient for the day is its own trouble."
Matthew 6:34

You cannot do anything about what will happen tomorrow. You have the choice to sit around and worry like crazy but this thinking will only stress you out and cause major anxiousness. Do you really want to live that way? God doesn't desire that you think ahead to a yet-to-happen hypothetical situation and worry until you're weary. In this verse Jesus reminds you that tomorrow will worry about its own things. Therefore, commit tomorrow into His hands and be stress-free today as you trust God.

Anxiety will arise when we begin to worry about the future and the handful of outcomes that *could* happen. How many times have we thought about future scenarios and we begin to tense up because, *what if those things happened?* Usually those possible future outcomes that we worry about will never ever come to pass. So how should we, as believers, view the future and what attitude are we to convey about tomorrow? First of all, being a Christian, we must know and have faith in the fact that God will provide for us and sustain our lives every day. The hardest and most blessed action to take is to simply trust God.

If things seem overcomplicated, it may be because you are overthinking and overanalyzing. Yes, we are to use our minds and think things through but we have to remember *not* to overthink scenarios that are yet to happen. The devil loves and lives for a couple things—for Christians to be inactive in their faith and to drive doubt into our minds and lives. He thrives off of bringing discouragement to us in order to crush our countenance. Yet, the Lord assures us over and over that He is in control and He will take care of our tomorrows. Assurance will replace anxiety when our eyes are upon God's promises and heart toward His children. Be confident in His promises.

> From God's view, our tomorrow is already taken care of so that we can fully focus on today.

What we focus on the most will consume our lives and time. When the future is our focus and it takes away from the present, then it's time to readjust our thinking. In the past I've been so future-focused that I missed out on what God was presently doing in my heart and life. The result of overly thinking about tomorrow is that we cease to acknowledge the amazing feats that the Lord is doing right now!

Have you ever been spending time with someone and instead of being all there you were worrying about that thing you have to do tomorrow? Let's not do that anymore. I don't want to sacrifice quality time in the present with people that matter for hypothetical situations that probably will never happen. Worry about the future causes major stress that will steal away our joy. When we truly live in the now, realizing God is providing for us at this very moment, we will not let the worry of tomorrow tear us apart.

Corrie Ten Boom, a Holocaust survivor and avid believer, said, "Worry does not empty tomorrow of its sorrow. It empties today of its strength." Embrace where God has you presently and be confident that you are in His hands. Let your doubts die, your worries wash away and your stress sink into the sea. When it comes to provision, be fearless knowing that the Father has you in His loving hands.

Walk confidently in Christ, having faith that He will make a way and lead the way for your tomorrow. Don't worry about what you can't control; instead have a heart of worship for what God has done in the past and is doing in your life now. You can praise God because of His present provision. God will take care of your tomorrow as you just keep seeking Him today and look to Jesus in every and all situations. Let Him consume every part of you. Wherever He has you currently, you can be confident He will give you all you need, so praise Him and thank Him for right now.

DAY 11
CAST YOUR CARES

"Therefore humble yourselves under the mighty hand of God, that He may exalt you in due time, casting all your care upon Him, for He cares for you." 1 Peter 5:6-7

God has not called you to let pride fill your heart or drive your life. If you are a believer, you realize that life doesn't revolve around you; rather, life is all about the Lord and what He wants and wills. As you live your life for eternity, remember that God absolutely cares for you and desires that you let go of your worries and fears and give them over to Him. Your Creator is mighty and more than capable of lifting you up as you submit to Him. When you remain lowly, then God can shine brightly.

Humility results from laying pride aside and acknowledging that we need to be completely dependent upon our God. Oftentimes the more independent an individual becomes, the more unchecked pride resides in his heart. Pride does not have a positive track record. Back in high school I knew a kid who had so much pride in everything he did. He was overly confident and he did exceptionally well in all the activities he engaged in, becoming super popular. As time went on, I saw clearly that his pride led to a blinding factor that caused him to seriously struggle and fall. To this day he is adrift in life, disillusioned by his own haughtiness. I feel so sorry for him seeing that the outcome of pride is grief, loneliness and darkness.

This verse teaches me that humility correlates to a lack of worry. As we humble ourselves and exalt the Lord, our worry begins to wane and we enter a heart rest because we understand that God is in complete control. Humility is the awareness that we are completely weak and depleted of any substantial strength without the Lord. Humility reflects the reality that we are in desperate need of God's leading on an everyday basis. Philosopher and theologian Augustine said, "If you plan to build a tall house of virtues, you must first lay deep foundations of humility." We can't do it ourselves and if we try, we will fail. When this transparent fact rises to the surface of our minds, we will then come to the conclusion that God can and desires to carry us through. As we revel in the extreme love of the Lord in helping us with every concern that we have, we understand how deeply He cares for us and fear will quickly flee from our minds and hearts.

> To humble ourselves isn't a suggestion; it's a necessary action that should lead to the essential depletion of self-reliance.

When a person *casts* something, it means they are projecting it far away from them. This verse clearly directs the believer to cast their cares toward God. Will God take our cares and save them for us for a future date? Of course not! As we cast our cares upon the Lord and give over our worries to Him, He will take those cares and annihilate them, never to bring them up ever again! Our problem is that we take those cares back and our flesh wants to hold onto them because if we are not worried, something is wrong. I do not believe the Lord wants us to take any ownership over irrational worry. Don't let unfounded concerns build up in your mind. It's time to throw those concerns so far away from you that they are not even visible.

Don't fret about giving your worries over to the Lord! When we throw our burdens upon God, even those cares we've been harboring for years, the weight of that stress is sent away for good and forever. God is in no way weighed down by taking our cares upon Himself. Your Father in heaven is so mighty that He makes your cares look minuscule and totally inconsequential. He can handle every single ounce of pressure that you are presently facing because He is God and you are not. Cast *all* your cares upon God, for He cares for you.

DAY 12
NO FEAR

"The LORD is my light and my salvation; whom shall I fear? The LORD is the strength of my life; of whom shall I be afraid?" Psalm 27:1

When the Lord is your salvation, you are set free of fear. No longer do you have to fear death, darkness or destruction, or worry what man can do to you. Even if you were to be put to death, that is simply the gateway to eternity with the Lord! Being afraid becomes a foreign concept in your mind because you are filled with courage from your Creator constantly. Let the Lord be your strength, let Him fight your battles and let Him defend you always.

When we began following Christ, the light made the darkness dissipate. Aren't we blessed that God saved our souls and set us on the path illuminated by His Word and His will? I am absolutely overwhelmed, in a good way, that God grabbed my heart and changed my life! A few of my friends that I used to run with have died in recent years. A high school friend died in his sleep from drug overdose. Other friends have died tragic deaths; a couple of old friends had gone to prison for serious crimes. When I find out about these things, it makes me sad because those were people I used to hang out with, have fun with and were close friends with! At the same time I am overwhelmingly grateful that God pulled me out of the pit of this world and set me upon the Rock. I could have landed in prison or be dead by now if I had continued down the same dark path.

God is so faithful and His strength can steer your heart away from any and all fear. Because we know the Lord Jesus and are living to follow Him, we are saved from any and all eternal danger! Yes, we face earthly danger, conflict and opposition, difficulties and trials, but the Lord is on our side. That is enough to dispel all fear.

> Being scared becomes a foreign concept when we realize God is our courage.

The Lord is our strength in this life so we don't have to worry about getting through terrible trials. Bible teacher Woodrow Kroll said, "With the power of God within us, we need never fear the powers around us." We can confidently know that we will get through because God is the strength that propels us forward to spiritual progression. He is the One who lifts us up and equips us to face what other people would be afraid of. You and I are called to be bold in this life for no one and nothing can harm us because we belong to God!

The Bible says in Deuteronomy 10:12, "What does the LORD your God require of you, but to fear the LORD your God, to walk in all His ways and to love Him, to serve the LORD your God with all your heart and with all your soul." To fear the Lord means to stand in complete awe of who He is and wholeheartedly adore Him. When we understand that God is powerful and that He is capable of exerting His power to accomplish

His will, we will be left awestruck and in wonder of God's glorious plan! The Lord is our Creator and our leader in this life; therefore nothing can touch our soul. We simply fear and revere God as He uses His power to protect us eternally.

People may attempt to discourage you by filling you with fear of the future, but you can reject those ungodly thoughts and continue to fiercely follow after the Lord, letting Him fight for you. Do not let any person or situation intimidate you or cause fear to well up inside of you because you are the Lord's child. God is for you and He is on your side. He is in control and He is your strength in every single situation. Be fearless for you are a chosen child of God!

DAY 13
HIS PRESENCE

"For they all saw Him and were troubled. But immediately He talked with them and said to them, 'Be of good cheer! It is I; do not be afraid.'"
Mark 6:50

When Jesus is present in your life, you have no need to fear. As He speaks to you during trying times and various trials, you are reminded to remain calm and not be afraid. Many of your intense and difficult moments happen because of your focus getting misdirected. Those moments where you struggle often occur because all you see is the storm, the winds and the rain. The reality is that storms come and go but your Savior is there with you on the boat in the midst of the storm out at sea. His presence is with you always through every single life weather pattern. Take comfort in that!

In this verse, the disciples were troubled and afraid because they didn't recognize Jesus at first. As the disciples were in the boat, His followers saw a figure walking on the water and freaked out. The storm was raging and no doubt it was difficult to see clearly with the elements causing chaos around them. The disciples began to fear and stress out until they heard the voice of Jesus.

When I was a kid and I got hurt in some way, the voice of my parents totally comforted me in my pain.

Or when I was afraid of the dark, my Mom would rub my head and reassure me with her voice that everything was going to be OK. What followed was a peace as a young boy that eventually took my fear of the dark away. The voice of our Lord is there to lead us, calm our hearts and give us rest through extremely rough and unsettling times. Not only did Jesus calm the external storm, He also calmed their tumultuous hearts. The storms of life will rage, but the voice of Jesus brings true rest. Trouble arose when they didn't recognize Jesus, but when they heard His voice, the storm settled and the stress slipped away.

> The voice of the Lord will crush fear and conquer anxiety.

After He calmed the storm Jesus charged the disciples with encouraging words, "Be of good cheer." That's like saying to be joyful and have a good time during a hurricane. Isn't that kind of crazy?! Really, Jesus was reminding these guys they could be carefree because He was there and therefore, they didn't have to fret. Sometimes we begin to worry because we forget that there is sheer joy in the presence of Jesus! When God's presence is preeminent in our lives, the result will be a heightened countenance and abundance of joy. That sounds pretty amazing to me! Life can get us down, throw us curve balls and bring serious discouragement to our hearts. Circumstances can be bleak and dreary in this fallen, sin-scuffed world. But knowing that the Lord is always with us will result in a restful heart and a quiet peace. English preacher Thomas Watson said, "If God be our God, He will give us peace in trouble. When there is a storm without, He will make peace within. The world can create trouble in peace, but God can create peace in trouble."[5]

Keep in mind that there is no need for you to be troubled or terrified by life's circumstances. Storms may rage in your heart and trials may threaten your countenance now and then but remember that God is with you through it all! Therefore, you have to remember and recognize His presence, which will immediately bring an otherworldly solace and a supernatural peace to your heart. When you are in the midst of a dark storm, realize that Jesus is in the midst of your situation. Do not focus on the waves or wind, look to the Lord for peace and relief. Let fear drift out to sea and joy fill your heart for His presence will bring complete peace.

---

[5] Thomas Watson, *Gleanings from Thomas Watson*. (Grand Rapids, MI: Soli Deo Gloria Publishers), 1997..

DAY 14
NOT ALONE

"The LORD is on my side; I will not fear. What can man do to me? The LORD is for me among those who help me; therefore I shall see my desire on those who hate me." Psalm 118:6-7

The Lord is on your side and stands with you. The Lord is the One who crushes fear and decimates anxiety! His Word fills you with hope and encouragement. There will be those who will come against you and hate you, but don't let that affect you or pull you down. You were created to love the unlovable and tell truth to the world! Receive God's encouragement and keep going!

Sometimes in life we go through crazy conflicts. In those instances we come to realize who our true friends are. Those who do not stand by our side as we go through turmoil are often the ones who don't truly care about us. The fact that should always uplift us is that God cares for us so much! We go through these instances where we mistakenly think that no one cares about who we are, and so we feel alone in this life. We begin to get down on ourselves and feel like no one is with us or for us on planet earth. Then the Lord intervenes and enters our life and we are filled with reliable hope.

Before walking with the Lord, I felt so helpless; without meaningful direction for my life or my future.

In other words, I was lost and I desired so badly to be found. God began placing people in my life who shared with me of the true hope in Jesus Christ. And honestly, I didn't want to hear it. I was searching so hard for hope and yet the hope presented to me sounded foolish and I just didn't believe it, at first. But then the Holy Spirit began working radically in my heart and drew me to search out the things of God on my own. The truths I found literally changed my life and gave me a whole new perspective and outlook. I realized that He's not only with us always, but He also takes action in our times of trouble. Psalm 46:1 beautifully illustrates this point—"God is our refuge and strength, a very present help in trouble." The Lord helps and leads us on the mountaintops and in the valleys. He is there when things are smooth and He is there when things seem rough and rocky.

> Fear will stop our spiritual progress but faith will cause far-reaching spiritual progression.

After I began walking with the Lord, my aloneness dissipated. God's presence filled that annoying, lonely and darkened void. He is with us and for us in every season, in every scenario and every step of the way. Therefore, we have no need to fear about God abandoning us or leaving us out to dry. At one point in the apostle Paul's ministry, everyone scattered, leaving him alone. Not a single person stood with him when the pressure was on for living out his faith. Yet, Paul acknowledged that the Lord was with him and would never leave him! Our God is so good that He stays close when our circumstances are far from comforting. He is our constant help in trouble.

You can be fearless knowing that the Father is with you right now, interceding for you through your uneasy situations. He is there when no one else stands by your side, when those you thought were your friends have taken off. God is loyal and His presence is there to comfort your heart and reassure your soul.

Know that you are *not* alone. Even if there is hate toward you from others, God's love for you is all that truly matters and all that you need to focus on. People will enter and exit your life but the Lord has staying power! He will always be there for you. His love is powerful enough to fill your heart and lift your countenance for the rest of your days on this earth.

DAY 15
CRUSH FEAR

"I sought the LORD, and He heard me, and delivered me from all my fears." Psalm 34:4

As you seek the Lord, He hears your prayers and settles your heart. If you simply ponder the fact that the Lord of the universe listens to your personal pleas, you will be astounded and totally awestruck. Not only does God hear your prayers, He takes away all your fears as well. There's no validity to the idea that God isn't loving or gracious. He has the power to deliver you from every single one of your fears and all that pent-up anxiety. So place your life in His hands and watch God crush your fear!

Have you been struggling badly with fear and then you sought God and in seconds your fear vanished? That is how powerful and effective the Lord of the universe is! He doesn't want you to wallow in worry or be engulfed in timidity. He wants you to be delivered from the anxiety that follows fear. The enemy, on the other hand, wants you to be so filled with fear that you become inactive for the Lord and incapable of praise. The devil wants to stunt your spiritual growth to the point of separating you from your amazing God. With God's strength, resist the enemy and reach out to the Lord for He hears your prayers and wants to deliver you from the discouragement that the evil one brings.

The truth is as we draw near to God, He gives us a rest that is like nothing else in this world. Don't procrastinate in seeking the Lord for He knows everything that is on our heart and He wants us to commune and communicate with Him. Comfort comes and fear flees when we simply pray to God. It sounds so simple, doesn't it? But the truths of God and from God are amazingly profound and yet incredibly simple. Connecting to our Creator fosters faith and crushes fear. This is so imperative to grasp as believers. God's voice will validate our confidence in Him and give us victory over fear. Seek Him, hear Him and find comfort in Him.

> God wants to hear from you and He desires to kill your fear.

Life can get rough when there are reoccurring fears that fill our mind and anxieties that invade who we are. But as we seek God, He will grab and cast those fears away from us and we do not have to attempt to find them. Let God deal with your fears and anxieties! Fear is one of the weapons in the enemy's arsenal that he loves to use over and over again. But the weapons we have from the Lord lead to victory in every single struggle. The enemy's weak tactics are no match to our weapons—God's Word, prayer, and the power of the Holy Spirit. It's just a matter of using the weapons as we daily walk with God. We are conquerors because of our Creator. Corrie Ten Boom said, "The first step on the way to victory is to recognize the enemy." The enemy has no power to enslave us with irrational fear.

Peace comes from pushing your intense fears onto the Burden Lifter. In your life, as you stay close to God, the enemy will always lose and God will always win. God is strong enough to deflect the enemy's darts. You can find strength in Christ who will build barriers around you in order to block the enemy's entrance into your eternal destiny. Lean your whole weight onto the Lord and let Him fight your daily battles! Fling your fear toward the Father and He will take care of it and you can get genuine heart rest.

DAY 16
CALM AND QUIET

"In that day it shall be said of Jerusalem: 'Do not fear; Zion, let not your hands be weak. The LORD your God in your midst, the Mighty One, will save; He will rejoice over you with gladness, He will quiet you with His love, He will rejoice over you with singing.'" Zephaniah 3:16-17

God wants to work mightily in your life. When fear threatens to break you down, His presence brings protection and peace to your mind and heart. Fear is no match for your Father in heaven. His power will flood you with love so that you can rejoice through it all. Do not fear the future nor the present because your Father has you; He holds you in His hands. Be brave, take heart, and be confident in Christ. Let your faith dissolve your fear.

Some would postulate that if you are struggling, you don't have enough faith and so you need to seek God more. Much of the time the judgers blame you for the troubles and difficulties you are facing when they're not your fault. Job's friends kept blaming his troubles on Job himself even though he kept the faith through serious hardships! These actions are not of God. Oftentimes we struggle because there is a lot of conflict and difficulty in the world that is beyond our control. One of the reasons we should look to the Lord on a consistent basis is because we've given over control to Him so that, like the amazing Father He is, He takes care of our burdens! There will always be conflict and external inconsistencies in our lives, but our Father will always be forever with us.

I want to encourage you not to let conflict take over your mind or threaten to alter your attitude toward others. Reject the situations that attempt to lead you into a state of unfounded fear; instead walk by faith and let God fight your battles. Nehemiah understood this because in the midst of his calling, there was great opposition—mockers, haters, and those who were jealous of what He was doing. He understood that He could continue the work unobstructed because God was the One going before him and defending him. The Lord is always very present in every one of our predicaments. God is a soul-saver, a rescuer and a deliverer.

> Destroying fear and replacing it with faith is so easy for God.

It is incredibly comforting that the Lord actually rejoices with gladness over His people. Sometimes we mistakenly think that God is annoyed when we come to Him, but that is never God's heart. He absolutely loves us and rejoices and sings over us like a caring parent to their precious child. The Lord protects us and quiets us with His love when our hearts are erratic and inconsistent. Sometimes our mind is far from quiet as it races chaotically, welling up with a multitude of fears, worries and anxieties. As humans we've wasted time worrying over possible events and hypothetical situations that probably would never come to pass. When we are in this anxiety-ridden state, we realize we are weak, but we also are reminded that God is strong. We get to throw our entire selves upon the Lord who holds us up and comforts our hearts. The moments in my life where I fully surrendered all that I am to the Lord were the moments I leaned my whole heart upon my heavenly Father. Lean upon your Father and let Him be your mighty protector and your great comforter. He is mighty to love. C. S. Lewis said, "Though our feelings come and go, His love for us does not."[6]

Your troubled heart can revert to calm and quiet when you believe the Lord is mighty to rescue you out of your dark and dreary fears. His hand is perpetually extended, reaching down and waiting for you to extend your hand up to Him so He can pull you out of the miry clay and set you upon the rock. He wants to take hold of your daily fears and gate them off, placing a do-not-enter sign on that area. Fear is never of the Lord but true faith proceeds from God. You have a measure of faith in the core of who you are and as you actively work out that faith, you will not have room in your heart for fear to live there. God rejoices over you and loves you too much to leave you knee-deep in fear. Your heavenly Father desires that you walk through this life unhindered, carefree and rejoicing on a regular basis. God is in your midst. Embrace the truth that the Lord uses His strength and might to turn your tumultuous heart into calm waters.

---

[6] C. S. Lewis, *Mere Christianity* (New York, NY: HarperOne), 2015.

DAY 17
ONLY BELIEVE

> *"As soon as Jesus heard the word that was spoken, He said to the ruler of the synagogue, 'Do not be afraid; only believe.'"* Mark 5:36

When you have faith, fear is an afterthought. When your focus is on fear, faith is an afterthought. Believing that God is carrying you and protecting you in and through this dark world will result in your faith flourishing and rising to the surface of your heart. The Lord desires that fear be ousted from your life and that you walk with confidence in God as He is all-powerful. Rise up and walk by faith and watch your fear diminish and disappear.

In today's verse, Jesus makes it clear to the ruler of the synagogue that he had no need to fear. The simplest way to make sure fear is made void is to set our eyes and mind upon the Victor. Distraction comes when we lose sight of the focal point and purpose of this life! During earthquakes, for instance, it is said that if we were to focus on one fixed point above, we would remain stable. There's a story about an intense earthquake that occurred in the midst of an evening gathering on a terrace. Everyone was falling down and hurting themselves during the huge quake, except for one man. This guy immediately looked up and fixed his eyes on one shining star and was able to remain completely stable during that chaotic moment. When our eyes are fixed on Jesus, no amount of intense life situations will cause us to fear or fall.

The ruler of the synagogue was told a harsh reality—his daughter had passed away. Jesus lovingly and pointedly tells this man not to be afraid but only believe. It seems so elementary to have faith when we are afraid. Yet, so often we forget about faith, and then fear begins to overwhelm our lives. It is our faith in the Lord that keeps us confident in Christ and guarded through any and all grief. Faith stems from fully believing in the promises of God. The ruler's twelve-year-old daughter came back to life as Jesus took the child by the hand and lifted her up.

Faith is the catalyst that dissolves fear.

When God gives us a command, we don't have to worry that He is leading us astray or giving false information. We can wholeheartedly believe. Jesus told the ruler that having faith in the works of the Lord means being so sure of God's words that fear is torn away and replaced with trust. One of the ways to build trust is to look at the track record of those who have come through for us in the past. Those who have been and remained dependable can be trusted because they were reliable time after time. Our God is trustworthy and as we continue to seek Him, we will trust Him more and more.

A healthy spiritual habit to implement as believers is to look up often and lean upon God regularly. When my heart is unsure or unsettled, I often go to the Word of God to remind myself of those verses that always calm my heart and give me solace in the midst of my anxiety-laden situation. It works every time because God's Word never brings turmoil; it always brings peace and assurance. Soak in the Scriptures and remind yourself of His great promises. When you place your faith in the Promise Keeper and plow ahead, you will be lifted up. I love God's Word so much!

As you trust in the Lord, your disposition is leveled off with total peace through problematic situations. God has the capacity and great power to cut off your fear from the forefront of your life. If you overthink about possible negative life outcomes, those thoughts will flood your heart with stress and worry. Be willing to give up your fear to the One who can calm your heart continually. Surrender every single one of your fears to your Almighty God. Cast them toward Him! The Lord never calls you to be afraid, timid and depleted of courage. Never. God can take away your fear and fill you with faith the very moment you ask Him to. There's no doubt that when your eyes are upon the Lord, your heart will be flooded with faith and freed from worry. The Lord is all the encouragement you need.

DAY 18

DON'T BE TROUBLED

"But even if you should suffer for righteousness' sake, you are blessed. And do not be afraid of their threats, nor be troubled." 1 Peter 3:14

The possibility of suffering should not make you shy away from doing God's work. There are times when you will get in trouble for doing what is aligned with God's ways. You will sail through storms, track through trials and head into hardships because of your faith, but don't lose heart! Experiencing pushback for your faith demonstrates that you are not ashamed to shine the light of the truth into this dim world. As you follow the Lord, there will difficulties due to living out your faith. But please realize that those moments of difficulties are monumental because God is pleased when you live boldly for Him!

When hardships happen, we can count ourselves blessed and actually have joy! We don't ask for suffering nor do we ever want to be rejected for what we believe, but when these things happen, we can rejoice as our confidence is in being about our Father's work. I've had friends who, after I was saved, would not ever contact me or return my calls. They thought I was being all weird talking about Jesus, going to church and reading the Bible. I attempted to stay in contact with them to share my faith but I was rejected by a few of them. It was difficult for me at first but the more I sought God and grew in my faith, the more I came to the realization that it was quite normal for the believer to experience both influence for the faith and rejection for the faith. Throughout the years I had friends who were believers who thought I was too outspoken about my Christian life. Yet, I'm not called to be quiet or timid in the Lord, I'm called to shine the light of Christ boldly and unashamedly! Some will accept Christ, others will reject Christ. But either way, I'm called to be upfront about the gospel and courageous in my faith.

We are called to live out what God has laid out.

We never need to be afraid of threats that come as a result of our faith in Christ. Even the most vicious and angry Christian hater can do nothing to your soul and can do nothing to break down what God has built up within you. We aren't living to please people, nor are we living to fear people. Our daily and primary focus is Jesus, no matter what! We don't ever need to be anxious about what others will do or say because we are bold in our walk with God. People need to understand that faith isn't just something that we do, it makes up who we are. When we stand up for what we believe, hate will be hurled our way by those who are against God, but at the same time, we will influence those who are genuinely hungry for truth.

Count yourself blessed if you receive pushback for publicly praising the Lord for God is pleased with your boldness! Don't be troubled with those who ridicule you for your right standing with God because the Lord may be breaking through their angry heart and working in radical unseen ways!

May the hatred that could come your way for living out your faith not affect your witness for Christ, but may it cause your heart to burn for lost souls even more. When you stand firm in your faith, fear will not fall upon you and timidity will never trample you. In sharing the gospel, we are not looking for a fight; we are simply walking by faith as we look to Jesus. It pleases God when you live a life that is reflective of the Lord's heart. As you suffer for righteousness sake, you are blessed because your boast is in Jesus Christ.

DAY 19

OVERARCHING PEACE

"And when I saw Him, I fell at His feet as dead. But He laid His right hand on me, saying to me, 'Do not be afraid; I am the First and the Last.'"
Revelation 1:17

When you revere the Lord, you will have the right outlook and perspective on life. As God is sovereign over what you do and where you go, the result on your part should be an awestruck obedience. God is powerful and as you follow Him, you will clearly see His power at work making your faith soar! It's OK to allow yourself to be pleasantly overwhelmed at who God is and what He can do. As you take the Lord seriously, you will be walking toward the direction of your divine destination.

The glory of God really can be greatly overwhelming. John was extremely awestruck by the amazing vision he experienced in the book of Revelation. As he saw Jesus in His heavenly glory, John fell at His feet like a dead man. What a perfect reaction to seeing the glory of the Lord! Back in the day, when you saw a king or if you were summoned by a ruler, you'd bow at his feet in honor, respect and reverence. This was an outward demonstration that you were recognizing that the king was in charge and you were not. This is really a picture of our relationship with the Lord Jesus. He is in charge and we are not!

I've worked at certain companies where I was the manager, but I had one employee who acted like he was the manager. He ordered people around and would make decisions without consulting me first. I had to have a talk with this employee because some of the things he was saying were totally wrong and I had to correct his actions. He needed to be reminded that there was an order to this company and we were all required to follow that order and be content in our roles within the context of the job. He totally understood and everything was a blessing after that interaction.

Jesus is in charge and we are His children who willingly and lovingly follow Him! We are privileged to fall at the Lord's feet in worship and adoration because of who He is. We can praise Jesus by depending upon Him for everything that we go through and all that we face. What happens next is the action that would calm John down from his overwhelmed state. Jesus put His hand on John telling him not to be afraid. One touch from Jesus will torch any and all fear that we feel. If we are overwhelmed, let's be positively overcome by the overarching peace that Jesus brings.

> **Awestruck obedience is the result of seeing the Lord Jesus for who He really is—our King.**

When Jesus is the constant in our lives, He instills in us godly confidence to walk according to His ways and adhere to His will. As we daily surrender to His plan, fear and worry will be wrecked and prevented from polluting our minds and invading our hearts. The truth that Jesus is with us should calm and console us no matter what external incidents we encounter.

The first time I went on a big roller coaster with my dad, I was *so* nervous. My palms were sweaty, I was shaky and felt a bit lightheaded as we waited in the line. When we got to the front and into the roller coaster car, I kind of felt like this might be my last moment on earth. We started to ascend up the steep climb and in my mind I was making my peace with God. I thought, *I had a good run and now it will be over.* The roller coaster arrived at the top and began to descend superfast! Immediately my fear turned into unbridled laughter as I screamed with excitement the rest of the ride! I had never burst out laughing and screaming with joy so much in my life! It was amazing how quickly my fear turned into such memorable and exhilarating moment!

The Lord Jesus can disintegrate your fear in an instant as you simply trust Him. We are just along for the ride. You and I are not called to attempt to drive our lives or strive to steer our destiny in a certain direction. We let the Lord lead and sit back and enjoy every moment of where God is leading us. As you allow yourself to be awestruck by Jesus, He will take care of your life, so you don't have to worry ever!

May the Lord's overarching peace be so prominent in your life. As you live your life for the Lord, may you worry less and have joy more. Let Him crowd out any fear that has caused extreme chaos in your life. Fear is not from above and God does not want you to wallow in worry or allow fear to infiltrate your mind. Find comfort and solace from your Savior! Fear cannot touch a child of God who has potent and prominent faith.

DAY 20
SAVED FROM SINKING

"Say to those who are fearful-hearted, 'Be strong, do not fear! Behold, your God will come with vengeance, with the recompense of God; He will come and save you.'" Isaiah 35:4

Have you had moments when fear has gripped you? Has worry wrecked your plans as your mind focused on all the things that could possibly go wrong? Has anxiety taken over and you started freaking out because of some events that may happen but probably won't? Take heed to the words of Isaiah who reminds the people to be strong and not fear. God will save! This is a truth that you, as a believer, can count on, not just once in a while but every single day. Your God will fight your battles, defend you and protect you. Don't doubt that.

Strength and fear will never coincide. What fear does is steal our strength resulting in burdensome stress and intense anxiety. Fear is a feeling that stems from the situations and circumstances we encounter in this life. We forget that there's a whole unseen realm at work as we go about our day-to-day business.

When I was a new believer, I saw some people struggle with spiritual warfare and I thought that was really weird. I just didn't get it. But as I kept walking with the Lord year after year, I understood and the spiritual realm became clear to me. It is amazing to walk with the Lord, pray, read His Word and see Him do the miraculous. On the other hand, it is difficult, oppressive and dark when the enemy attempts to trip the Christian up. The spiritual realm is real, but so is the strength of our God! We need to wake up to the power we have in Christ. Our strength does not come from what is around us or within us, our strength falls from above! Our strength stems from the faith that God has ingrained in us. The Lord is the One who halts the opposition and oppression that targets and terrorizes us. God does the work and all we have to do is ask.

The enemy is a weakling but our God is mighty.

God is our rescuer who pulls us out of the fire and sets us in a safe space. He is our lifeguard who saves us out of the tumultuous waters and keeps us from sinking. He is our physician who heals our wounds; our leader who absolutely loves us and comforts our anxious hearts when things are falling apart. The Lord knew we needed a Savior to set us free of the fear of death, darkness and destruction. We all needed to be rescued and resuscitated spiritually. I am so thankful that the Lord gets me through life's difficult situations and sustains me on my God-given journey.

Bible teacher Warren Wiersbe wrote, "The safest place in the world is in the will of God, and the safest protection in all the world is the name of God." Fear is flushed out when we realize the magnitude of our Maker's love for us. Worry is washed away as we worship the King with all that's within us. Uneasiness is eradicated as we draw close to our Comforter.

You may not have had an ideal upbringing or your parents may have neglected you. But now that you are a believer, your Father in heaven loves you and wants to take care of you; He desires to be involved in your life and give you all you need to walk strong.

Know and believe that you can be free of fear and anxiety. You can be saved from sinking into those deep, dark depths, not by swimming but by surrendering to God. Raise your hands and let your Lifeguard pull you out of the water and set you on the dry deck of the boat. Let Him dry you off, speak encouragement and restore your heart. God will carry you through the waters and get you through the rough weather. Let Him take control. Let Him extract discouragement and instill His encouraging words into the core of who you are. You will find strength in your Savior as you stay on board and let God direct the course of your life!

DAY 21

UNDOING FEAR

"For I am persuaded that neither death nor life, nor angels nor principalities nor powers, nor things present nor things to come, nor height nor depth, nor any other created thing, shall be able to separate us from the love of God which is in Christ Jesus our Lord." Romans 8:38-39

God's love is the force that protects your heart and assures your mind. There are forces that threaten to lure you away from the Lord but those forces fall flat in the face of God's love. When you allow the love of God to truly penetrate the core of your being, your eyes will be open to the one and only valid reality— His love holds you and keeps you safe. His love brings comfort and cohesion. God is love and His love is directed toward you and it will never end.

Being united with Christ will flush fear out of our daily lives and bring confidence to the surface. In the workplace we all have known conceited and headstrong people. They walk over others to get ahead thinking they're the best person for any job or task. If you accomplish something, they would attempt to top that accomplishment by talking about how they accomplished something more amazing. Confidence in the Bible is not self-confidence, rather it's God-confidence. We are not self-promoting because our boast is in Christ. Knowing that Christ resides in our hearts brings a confidence that completely calms us in the most intense and unpredictable situation.

A calm heart results when our eyes are gazed upon the heavens and our hearts are bent toward eternity. We are saved and therefore, nothing can separate us from our Savior! Fear becomes part of the old life we've left behind. Being fearless stems from setting our affections on Jesus, the author and finisher of our faith (Hebrews 12:2). Sometimes we let our feelings get the best of us and we think God is distant or angry at us. He is not. He is right there with you, lovingly consoling and carrying you. Augustine said, "God loves each of us as if there were only one of us." Unity with Christ means the undoing of fear and the increase of faith. Christ unites us with the One who brings peace that surpasses all understanding (Philippians 4:7).

> Confidence occurs when we abandon self-focus and embrace Christ.

Death cannot come close to deterring us from our eternal destiny. Death is actually a gateway to our real home in heaven which the Lord Jesus is preparing for us. Before I began my walk with Jesus I feared death. I would just lie in my bed thinking how horrible it would be to die because there would be nothing but darkness. After I was saved I no longer feared death; it no longer has a hold on me. I'm seriously not worried about the day when my life ends on this earth because I know that my permanent home is not here but in heaven.

People often have questions about death, *Why do people die? Where do we go from here?* If only they knew that heaven contains more love and more beauty than we can ever fathom. Scripture says, "To be absent from the body and to be present with the Lord" (2 Corinthians 5:8). It means to be 100 percent healed from all the ails and ills of this world.

Intense life circumstances cannot lure us away from Christ who resides in us. No power can pull us away from the One who is in us. No created thing can disconnect us from our Lord. Understanding these realities will completely comfort our hearts and revolutionize our outlook on life. When fear creeps its ugly head into our minds, we can remember that Christ is with us fending off those feeble feelings of fear. Let Him fight for you!

Christ is with you, for you and in your heart to stay. There is literally no reason for you to worry about anything in this life. Sure, you can make a list of worries that seem valid, but the fact is that God never calls His kids to worry. Ever. It's time for you to undo fear because nothing in this world can separate you from the love of your Savior. Be confident in that.

DAY 22
FORGET EARTHLY FEAR

> *"You who fear the LORD, trust in the LORD; He is their help and their shield."* Psalm 115:11

When you have solid faith in God, you will be set up to trust God completely. You've been through some situations that have caused major fear and anxiety in your life and they have torn you apart. You've faced mountains that intimidated you and resulted in spiritual inactivity. You've given up and quit because of conflict. The beautiful truth is that as you fear the Lord and fully trust in Him, worry and anxiety will go from a present reality to a past testimony. You can have godly confidence that the Lord of hosts is your shield, your protector, and your strong tower.

Complete obedience to the Lord stems from a healthy fear of Him. The phrase *fear the Lord* should not freak you out or cause you to be scared that the Lord will take you out the next time you screw up. Fearing the Lord is such a healthy action for us to take as Christians! When the Bible exhorts God's followers to fear Him, the idea is not that we should be terrified of God because He is so intimidating and overarching, and at any moment your next screw up will be your last screw up. "Step back because here comes the bolt of lightning to destroy you!" No. The fear of the Lord means to see God in the right light and in the right way. We revere Him greatly because of what He has done, what He is doing, and what He is capable of.

It's critical to understand that He doesn't use His power to intimidate us, scare us, or cause fear in us. He uses His power to rejuvenate, restore, give grace and show mercy. He uses His power to love you! To fear God is to truly understand that He is God, and you are not! We worship Him with joy, but we also praise Him in adoration, devotion, commitment and total awe. To fear God is to have the right valuation of yourself—we don't see ourselves as amazing, God is amazing and we humbly submit to Him. To fear God is to put Him in His rightful place, on the throne of our hearts where He rules and reigns our everyday lives.

> God belongs on the throne, we belong at His feet.

The Lord has worked so powerfully in my life. I love when my day is laid out and I have my list of what exactly is going to happen each day. I love order and knowing what in the world will come next. When things start to interrupt that order and my list gets rearranged, I feel like I'm totally being tested. I understand that interruptions are often God's opportunities to work, but it is *not* easy. When a wrench is thrown into the system, then uncertainty ensues and panic brews. We don't like to be out of control and we do like to know what is going on in this life. But with the Lord, we *must* remain flexible if we are to walk by faith and grow in the faith. God is in control—and this we must remember often. Without intentionally doing it, we attempt to usurp the authority that God has! We run our race of faith behind Him, then come up next to Him and attempt to get ahead a little bit. That is when we trip up, fall and scrape our knees!

My youngest daughter, Lily, falls and scrapes her knees often because she's not paying attention or she doesn't let us help her. She cries and we pick her up and comfort her as she's weeping. When we are not paying attention and usurp God's lead, we will get hurt and then have to be comforted by our Father in heaven. Let's allow God to go before us and pay attention to what He is doing and how He is leading us. Knowing the Lord holds us in the palm of His hand should result in our hearts being engulfed with total peace. Fearing God is so freeing and relieving because it causes earthly fears to abate and dissipate instantly.

You can confidently stand in awe of God and adore Him for who He is. The Lord is sovereign. Fear will explode and come to nothing when you daily say, "God, please lead me today. You're in control. May I stay in the posture of simply following you." When you fear God, you will stick close to Him confidently through the mountains and deep dark valleys. Forget earthly fear by setting God on the throne of your heart and not edging your way onto the throne with Him. Stay at His feet. Stay humble. Simply follow.

DAY 23

GENUINE REST

"Cast your burden on the LORD, and He shall sustain you; He shall never permit the righteous to be moved." Psalm 55:22

If you carry your burden on your back, pretty soon you'll be crushed under its weight. God wants you to cast all your burdens at His feet! You never need to try and hold it all together yourself, for the weight will be too much and you'll fold under the pressure. As you live out your days with a solid trust in God, casting your burdens constantly on Him, you'll live a life that is peaceful and restful. The way to have genuine heart peace is by taking those worldly weights off your shoulders and giving them over to God. When you take this action, you will not be moved away from your God; instead you'll draw closer to Him.

Heavy burdens have no room to reside in the life of a believer. As burdens pile upon our shoulders causing unneeded stress, we are to throw them up toward the Lord. Here in the Deep South, people are legally able to have burn piles and they just light the fire on the pile to get rid of it. If they have trash and various things taking up space in their yard and they get to a point where it's time to make more space, they just burn the pile. Whatever burdens are attempting to occupy your heart, it's time to cast those things off into the fire and make space. You and I are not called to carry around burdens in this life. Ever! Yet at times we believe that it should be our job and task to carry these things that God has told us to cast upon Him. Throwing our burdens in the direction of our God will result in a relief that will keep us spiritually healthy.

Biblically, it is never God's intention to cast burdens upon us to weigh us down to the ground. He is not constantly testing us to see how much stress we can sustain. Today's verse makes it clear that God wants to free us of those unnecessary weights that bog us down and seize valuable space in our minds and hearts. Take your burdens to the Lord and leave them there for good. After all, Jesus makes it clear that His burden is light (Matthew 11:30).

Burdens are not meant to be carried by you.

How many times have you worried about events that never actually happened? Most of us spend way too much time stressing about things that will never occur. You look back and wonder why you ever worried in the first place! When my family and I moved from California to Alabama to plant a church, I didn't worry at first. I was so excited for this new adventure God was calling our family to! Everything was perfectly lining up as God gave us confirmation after confirmation. But then after we had been here a while and I was attempting to find a job to provide for my family, I could not find a job and I began to worry. I was striving to find work but doors remained closed on a daily basis. Finally I surrendered the burden of finding a job to the Lord and that was when God clearly led me to a place of employment through His divine hand. The only reason it was stressful and difficult was because I made it stressful and difficult. God didn't throw that burden on me, I had to cast the burden toward Him! He has our whole lives in His hands and in His control. The sooner we believe that and walk in that, the sooner we will be joyful and carefree! When our eyes are on our uneasiness because of unwanted difficulties, we will be moved in the wrong direction. Our goal is to constantly draw near to God and He will draw near to us (James 4:8). If we get caught up by the storms of this life, we will be consumed. When we let the Lord consume us, we'll get lifted up with Him. Let the Lord crush your burdens as you simply come to Him.

The Lord will sustain you as you journey through this sin-ridden world. He has the authority to make sure that you are not moved by stress and anxiety. He protects you and will not permit the enemy to get a leeway in your life. God brings genuine rest to your mind as you choose to surrender to Him daily. Cast your burdens upon God and watch Him absorb every heavy load you're carrying upon your shoulders. It will be so relieving!

DAY 24
SECURE IN HIM

"The fear of man brings a snare, but whoever trusts in the LORD shall be safe." **Proverbs 29:25**

You have no reason to fear anyone in this life. You are not called to let the fear of people dictate what direction to go or what attitude to have. Humankind does not have a say when it comes to your soul. People may attempt to intimidate you or cause fear to well up inside of you, but you have the choice to resist their feeble actions. God calls you to trust in Him. To have faith in God and fully trust Him is to lean on God with your whole weight, holding nothing back. As you lean toward the Lord and allow your life to please Him, fearing man will not even be a valid option!

Safety comes from setting our trust upon the Lord. I have friends who work in factories where they operate dangerous machinery. They are often telling me about how they have seen co-workers get into accidents and their hands and arms chopped off. Businesses like that have many safety requirements and they make sure to train and test every employee that works there. The employees are taught to trust the safety process. They must pay attention and take all the precautions to be safe! As believers we are taught that trusting God means to walk in the way He prescribes and to simply trust His leading.

Doing so will keep us safe and as a result, our minds off the fear of people.

At the end of his life, Solomon, after he had tried every worldly sin, learned that there were only two main commandments that led to a fulfilled life—fear God and keep His commandments. Notice how there is nothing about fearing man or worrying about what others think, or trying to please people? Yes, we aren't called to live like that. Fearing people's opinions or possible reactions toward us can hinder our walk with the Lord and cause us to focus on people instead of God. Man can do nothing to our soul, and that's a major reassurance! You and I get to live for the Lord and follow Him! If we fear people's outlook upon our life or calling, it could put an end to the Lord's work in our lives. Caring about what everyone else thinks could lead to an idleness in the Lord's work, and that's never good! Letting earthly fear into our world could very well stop spiritual progress in our lives. May we have no fear when it comes to man's opinion. May we fully fall upon the Lord with a reverent trust and an eternal expectation.

> You are never called to fear those around you. Instead, you are called to trust the Lord.

Fully having faith in the Lord will take away the fear of anything in this life. The more we fall upon the Lord in dependence, the more He will hold us up, lift us up and fill us up. Are you trusting in yourself too much? If you are fearful and anxious, it may be that you are leaning upon your own wisdom and your own ways! This whole devotional is about being fearless and we can be fearless as long as we give every single day to God! I used to have an acquaintance who trained a very well-known and successful UFC (Ultimate Fighting Championship) fighter. This ultimate fighter was a Christian; he loved the Lord and he fought in the name of the Lord. He was fearless and gave his all to the UFC. He often won and became really well-known! As we follow God, we can be extremely confident that He is in control and will ultimately give us the victory! No fear is sanctioned to reside in our heart or live in our life. Trusting in the Lord will expel any anxiety and worry that may creep in from the external world. Biblically, our souls are safe since we know the Lord and are secure in Him.

Now is not the time to hold back our faith or attempt to do life on our own without the Lord's leading. Forget fear by peering into the power of the Lords as He wraps His arms around us. He protects us and uses His power to pummel the darkness by shining His light. Set your mind upon the Lord so that the snare of fear will be obliterated. The harmful effects of fear will be turned off in your heart and mind when we turn on our trust in God. Have faith in the Father as He lovingly holds you through hardship, trials and storms. He has you and He is with you. Fearing man is not even an option when you realize and recognize how powerful and amazing your God is! Let fearlessness reign and remember that you are secure in Him.

DAY 25

FERVENT FAITH

"Let not your heart be troubled; you believe in God, believe also in Me." John 14:1

If we're being honest, we have had moments where our faith has wavered. Our heart has been unsettled and we've felt the brunt of the world's weight fall upon our shoulders. Times have been tough and life felt so uncertain. Yet Jesus reminds us, "Let not your heart be troubled." We don't have to be anxious as we go through rough roads and we don't have to crumble under the burdens we carry. As we believe in God, the weights are lifted and the troubles will not trip us up. Have fervent faith by leaning all our weight upon God.

I love when things in life just go smoothy and terrific circumstances fall into place. It's a blessing when we can say with assurance, "No worries" or, "It's all good." I'd choose sunny days over stormy seasons any day and anytime. When trouble invades our lives, it can tend to tear us apart and leave us feeling trampled down by life itself! In these times we live in, trouble can sneak into our minds at every turn if we are not focused on the Trouble Reliever. C. S. Lewis said, "God knows our situation; He will not judge us as if we had no difficulties to overcome. What matters is the sincerity and perseverance of our will to overcome them."[7] Difficult times truly cause us to

---

[7] C. S. Lewis, *Mere Christianity* (New York, NY: HarperOne, 2015).

live in a state of disorder and chaos as fear invades and faith seems to run out the door. With all of these external difficulties that attempt to align themselves with our lives, we have to remember where authentic peace emanates from. When we have faith in God alone, what will follow is peace of mind and heart. Fearlessness comes when we fall at the feet of Jesus and believe completely that He is the source of rest and the cradle of comfort.

When we have faith in God, peace will follow.

As believers, trouble should not be our focal point nor our constant companion. Trouble should be flicked off the table into the trash like a bread crumb. I do not believe that the Lord desires that we take on the troubles and cares of the world, nor does He want us to try and solve all of life's issues apart from Him! We need the Lord and we need to lean upon Him. Trouble will dissipate as we look to our Creator in day-to-day situations.

When we are fearful because of a dark trial, we must remind ourselves to just trust in the Lord. Stop complicating it. Keep it simple and look to your Savior! When we feel like we are stuck in a rut, believe in the Lord and lean upon Him with all of who you are. Your spouse is not your savior, your kids are not your savior, your job is not your savior. Jesus is your Savior!

When we feel like we have no hope, hold onto the Lord with a grip that cannot be breached. God seriously can turn those problems in your life presently into a peace that is real. He can transform those storms into serene waters in an instant. Simply believe in Him!

Pour your fervent faith into the Father and pay attention to Him. Keep yourself grounded in God's Word, worshipping Him and seeking Him in prayer. Your life is all about placing the Lord first and seeking to further His kingdom. The road of God's will isn't problem-free, there will be pushback and hardship. Even then, do not give up! Place your faith in the One who has given you life and freedom. Let go of fear and embrace Jesus. He loves you so much!

In the midst of the storm, realize that your Savior is right there, hand extended, ready to pull you aboard the boat and keep you safe and warm. Genuine faith in Christ will always lead to perfect peace.

DAY 26
BE FEARLESS

"For you did not receive the spirit of bondage again to fear, but you received the Spirit of adoption by whom we cry out, 'Abba, Father.'"
Romans 8:15

God never gives the OK for fear to be integrated into your life. You've been worried and stressed out in the past and you felt anxious and scared. You were unsure about what the future held and it did not look good. The reality is that God has adopted you into His family and you are accepted forever! What an amazing truth that should cause your heart to soar with comfort and relief. You were once Fatherless because you didn't know God and He felt far from you and distant, until He broke through your heart and opened your eyes. You're accepted and you are beloved.

It's so easy to allow ourselves to fall into bondage and spiritual confinement. Realize that faith is what eradicates the intense bondage that results from living in this bleak and broken world! The faith that God has given us is a gift that grows into spiritual protection. There are children out there who are neglected and abandoned. They long for parents who would adopt them and give them a chance so they can be in an environment where they are accepted. God is a Father who accepts those who have never been accepted and He loves those who have always felt unloved. Our Father in heaven is amazing!

> The enemy is weak; do not let him have a foothold in your life.

Statistics indicate the shocking fact that fear is leading the charge in breaking people down. Fear is not from above nor will it ever be. God isn't looking for opportunities to fill us with fear and to worry us about the next season of life we're traveling into. In the area of fear, the enemy is winning by luring people into the trap of insecurity. Fear is so extremely powerful that it can distract us from the race the Lord has us running. Yet, we have to remember that as we run our race of faith, the enemy will do everything he can to deter us from our purposeful path. The devil desires to destroy our countenance by triggering fear through our outward circumstances and life situations. The spiritual battle is real and continual in this life. We must resist the enemy by walking by faith on a day-to-day basis. To be fearless means to not let the world, the flesh and the enemy deter us from taking ownership of our calling. We must put both feet into the road of God's will.

When I was a kid, I used to love the game dodgeball. I remember as I would stand against the wall, I had to constantly watch and be aware of when the balls would be coming toward me. I had to sidestep and duck and run as fast as I could in that small space with boundaries. It took constant awareness to dodge what was thrown at me. Similarly, the Christian life takes a constant dodging of darts the devil hurls at you. We must watch and pray and be constantly aware that the enemy is waiting for a weak point or a soft spot so he can attack. We must raise up that God-given shield and not let arrows of anxiety penetrate the layer of courage the Lord gives. Like Nehemiah said, "Our God will fight for us" (Nehemiah 4:20). It's time to believe this and walk confidently in our God!

Cry out to the Creator who is calling you to draw near to Him. Be honest and transparent with the Lord and let His love lure you in and let His promises protect your heart in this troublesome world. The bonds of sin are broken when you truly believe in the Lord and fully depend on God. Lean into your Father and let Him carry you. God loves you and wants to daily lift you up, out of your rut and onto the Rock. It is a blessing to be integrated into God's big and diverse family. Seek God and walk with Him for He absolutely loves you! Let Him take your hand and fortify your heart as you simply follow Him. You will be accepted, loved and completely cared for.

DAY 27
A SETTLED HEART

> *"And when they saw Him walking on the sea, they supposed it was a ghost, and cried out; for they all saw Him and were troubled. But immediately He talked with them and said to them, 'Be of good cheer! It is I; do not be afraid.'"*
> Mark 6:49-50

You've been in seasons of life where you were not sure what God was doing. You could not see His plan for your life and it led to your discouragement. You sought Him and still you were troubled; yet you kept seeking Him in the storm. Finally the sun shone through the clouds and you could see the rain subsiding. These are such difficult moments to go through but they define your faith and refine your life. God does not waste the storm; rather He uses it as a great opportunity to teach you to fully trust in Him!

The unknown can result in a troubled heart and unsettled feelings. As the disciples of Jesus saw someone walking on the water and did not know who it was, they were gravely afraid. Have you ever been in circumstances that caused major worry and fear? We all have and it is never fun to be in a place like that! When we are in the rough and dark waters of life, we will face many unknowns. As much as we'd love to know what is going on in our near future, the reality is that we cannot predict and plan for every upcoming situation. It can be so difficult!

But then, a divine interruption occurs in the form of our Lord's comforting voice. When the disciples heard the voice of Jesus, they were amazed. The sheep know the Shepherd's voice even when storms threaten to drown out the Savior's assuring words. Even in the midst of distracting and chaotic noise, the Lord speaks so that our hearts can be settled and softened.

> One of the fastest ways to eradicate anxiety is to seek God and hear from Him.

There have been countless times in my life where the voice of the Lord was exactly what I needed to wash my worry away. The waves of God's encouragement wash over His kids bringing refreshment, clarity and heart rest. As the Lord has led me on His path from year to year, I've learned to let His voice be the loudest in my life. God has a calling for each one of us and He wants to use us greatly for His glory! When we walk in our calling, we will be on the road of His will and our hearts will be settled and our minds will be at peace. Jesus simply said to these guys, "Be of good cheer." When one fears, the last glimmer of joy will dissipate and discouragement will increase. But when our ears are open to God's voice, we will hear His promises and be encouraged as we set our minds on eternal realities rather than earthly tumult. Be still and listen for His voice in the midst of the storm. When you do, the storm will quiet down and you will hear the Lord's comforting words. Receive His encouragements to your very situation. No storm is too intense for God to handle. You can and should be fearless even in the midst of the chaos of life.

If you are overly focused on your earthly surroundings rather than on the Savior, you may sink in despair and waste time in anxiety. If you are focused on the Savior, even in the middle of the storm, you will stay afloat. You will hear God's voice in the most trying times of your life. So fear not, for God will give you words of encouragement and even give you reason to smile in the midst of the most intense storm! Be of good cheer and lean upon God and your heart *will* be settled!

DAY 28
WIPE OUT WORRY

"Then the angel said to her, 'Do not be afraid, Mary, for you have found favor with God.'"
Luke 1:30

Unexpected events will always happen in your life. Events that you did not plan for can easily bring fear into your heart and mind, if you let them. God works, but sometimes you wonder, *What in the world is He doing?* You may become worried, stressed or anxious because you don't like unexpected or unplanned things. Yet, if it's the Lord's will, you can fully trust that He knows what He is doing, way better than you! God has favor upon you and He wants the best for your life—and the best for your life is His plan and will.

God has ways of eradicating worry and destroying stress. He sent an angel to Mary to give her a message not to be afraid during a time of total uncertainty. Called by God to bring Jesus into this dark and bleak world, Mary was shocked and surprised and caught off guard. Yet, having heard from the Lord, she gained peace and followed through with His will for her. God sent an angel to alleviate her anxiety concerning His will.

You ever been there? You are caught off guard by how the Lord is moving and at first you freak out a bit. But then, as you seek God and clearly hear from Him, you are comforted and become confident in what He is doing. Often this is how God works; it takes our willing hearts to heed the Lord's perfect plan.

Evangelist George Müller said, "The beginning of anxiety is the end of faith, and the beginning of true faith is the end of anxiety." Anxiety can erupt in our lives if we don't remain flexible to the Lord's leading. He knows what He is doing and He definitely knows where we need to go and what we need to do! God will calm us through the calling He places on our hearts. The Lord will fully assure us as we align our lives with Him.

> Stay flexible to the Father because He knows what you need to do and where you need to go.

Finding favor with God equates to the absence of fear. There are so many people who have given in to fear and have fallen because of fear. God gives us the tools to stand firm in Him and gain His rest and peace—rather than letting our feelings dictate how we operate. If you are letting your feelings go unchecked, then you are heading in the wrong direction without knowing what is going on! If you want to end up lost, let your emotions lead you. If you want to stay on track, let the Lord lead you. God blesses those who walk by faith and keep focused on Him. Sometimes our view of ourselves can leave us discouraged and depressed. Yet, God's view of us will build our confidence in Christ simply because He loves us. The Lord's unfailing love causes fear to be forsaken and faith to be awakened! When we live fearlessly, we are living the way God intended us to live. When we see ourselves as God sees us, we will rise up boldly, be favored highly and be incredibly joyful.

Christian maturity is all about trusting the Lord's hand in your life. Uncertainty can be undone and fear can be avoided by simply staying close to the Lord. How is your relationship with Him? Are you delving into His Word on a regular basis and seeking Him through prayer? As you stay connected to your Creator, you will be called to certain tasks and missions and He will enable you to live out your calling. God favors you and loves you. May this truth lift up your countenance and give you a courage that will crush fear and wipe out worry. May you live without fear knowing God has a great plan for your life.

DAY 29
FOREVER FEARLESS

"Watch, stand fast in the faith, be brave, be strong." 1 Corinthians 16:13

You can't be sincerely brave and strong without the Lord. As you live out your purpose, God will give you the faith, bravery and strength you need for every situation you will face. Fearlessness should be a key characteristic in your life and there is absolutely no reason to let fear seep into who you are. The source of strength is your God in heaven! Seek Him and you will be equipped with strength and bountiful in bravery. The Lord will never call you to be fearful but He will always call you to be fearless.

There are many worries and anxieties that emanate from unexpected situations. Does anyone really enjoy unforeseen circumstances that can change your whole week? I don't think so. I love living by a schedule, and when that schedule changes it's rarely convenient. Routine brings comfort and to-do lists bring order. Yet in His omniscience the Lord will change things up, especially when our plans are not aligned with His will!

To be fearless, we need to be aware of life circumstances that produce fear. Worldly events can cause some serious anxiety and fear in our minds. When we are aware of those fears that come from external circumstances, we will be able to stand firm in the faith. To watch means to be awake to those anxieties that can creep into our lives. We must fight against all fears by standing strong in the Lord. Bravery doesn't come from within, it comes from above as the Lord equips us with pure boldness that fosters unstoppable faith.

I learned years ago that I have nothing to fear because I'm walking with the Lord. He leads us and is with us even in the darkest of valleys. When my eyes are upon the circumstances of this world, things grow dark and bleak and really hopeless. But when my eyes are focused on things above, I become confident in Him and my fear fades completely.

Seek the Lord constantly and fear will flee.

The enemy will continually attempt to tear away any faith and strength the Lord has instilled in you. He is relentless but weak and powerless in comparison to our Almighty God! We are not called to be passive when it comes to facing fears and fighting for the faith. So I'm not just going to sit back and let the enemy have a field day on my mind and life. He will speak lies to me, but those lies will have no effect if I am constantly sticking to the truth.

Corrie Ten Boom, whose family helped many Jews escape from the Nazis during the Holocaust in World War II by hiding them in their home, said, "The first step on the way to victory is to recognize the enemy." When it comes to walking by faith, we need to be proactive, and the result will be strength, bravery and major perseverance. When we are depleted of all earthly energy, we are to fall upon the Lord who will fill us with His strength and stamina. We can be brave in this world knowing that the Lord is in control of our situations.

May we be fearless as we tap into the strength of our God in those moments of debilitating weakness. God is our strength through the storm; our shield through the rain. He is the reason we can stand fast while in this shaky, unstable world and He is the One who grows us in the faith. We can trust Him to bless us with all we need to lead a victorious Christian life. Be confident in Christ so that fear is a thing of the past. Walk in victory and resist the vices that lure you away from the Lord. Stand firm in the Lord who absolutely loves you. Be forever fearless.

DAY 30
GOD IS WITH YOU

> *"Yea, though I walk through the valley of the shadow of death, I will fear no evil; for You are with me; Your rod and Your staff, they comfort me."* Psalm 23:4

Are you walking through some dark valleys feeling like God has deserted you? Does it seem like there is no help in sight? You may have felt hopeless, but know this: God is always with you and He will never leave you. When you realize that God is with you in the difficult valleys, and on clear mountaintops, you will live a fear-free life. When you know you are protected and safe, you will be at ease in any situation. This is the hope that we believers always have!

As we navigate through this dark world, we have no need to fear. We can either look at our surroundings and become paranoid or we can look to the Lord and be at peace. As for me, I am not going to live in fear and let my circumstances dictate the direction I go in life. Living in fear would be a complete waste of time and a guarantee that I'd end up lost in the woods. I want to follow the Lord and let Him direct me every step that I take. To live in fear is also a waste of joy. God actually wants His kids to be joyful, enjoying His undeserved blessings!

When I was blessed to go to Israel and see many biblical sights, I felt so safe. Even though Israel is a target and has many enemies, there are a multitude of armed guards all throughout the city making sure everyone is safe! I felt safer in Israel than in America! It's important to realize and remember that our perfect God is protecting us every step of the way in this bleak and dreary world. We will all experience times where we go through deep valleys, but even then the Lord is leading us and looking out for us.

> The fact that God is so close to His kids should bring a comfort and assurance that nothing else in this universe will bring.

God's presence gives a freedom from fear that helps us to forge ahead in the faith. Don't you want to forge ahead in the faith instead of backtracking on your spiritual journey? Sure God's protection is invisible, but that doesn't discount the fact that we are protected constantly—He guides and guards us even from the infiltration of evil into our minds and lives.

A shepherd's rod and staff were tools of protection for the sheep to fend off enemies that attempted to lure the sheep away. Even in the deep valleys, the Lord makes sure we are perfectly safe as He goes before us and watches out for us. He secures our soul by bringing complete comfort to our hearts. We can be at rest even in the darkest night knowing that our Good Shepherd is with us and looking out for us. His eyes are upon us as He protects our soul from sinking into this fallen world.

Stick close behind the Lord as circumstances and situations can cause intense fear within you. Allow

God to grab that fear and rip it away from your mind, heart and life. You have no reason to worry as your loving God is with you through every season of your life. His presence really does bring you peace and protection, a fearlessness that will build in you a boldness that falls from above. Let God's love replace your fear with faith. God's with you now and forever. Receive God's protection and know that He is surrounding you even now. Breath and be relieved. Amen.

CONCLUSION

This devotional is all about being fearless in the midst of a dark and dreary world. Being a child of God is such an amazing thing because you don't have to let fear dictate your actions and decisions. Feelings don't take precedence over faith. God wants you to walk through this life confident in Him because He is with you and will always be with you.

Many times in my Christian life I have succumbed to fear. Looking back in hindsight, I've realized that there is literally nothing to fear because God is not a fair-weather Father. He is faithful through it all, every step of the way. He has me and is with me and is constantly leading me. The same is true for you!

My prayer is that you would walk by faith so that fear will never get a foothold in your life. Live a life of assurance and confidence because the Lord is always there for you. Walk by faith and let fear fall.

Made in the USA
Middletown, DE
15 May 2022